# VALUE MANAGEMENT

*Creating
Competitive Advantage*

# VALUE MANAGEMENT
## Creating
## Competitive Advantage

J. JERRY KAUFMAN

CRISP PUBLICATIONS

Editor-in-Chief: *William F. Christopher*

Project Editor: *Kathleen Barcos*

Editor: *Regina Preciado*

Cover Design: *Kathleen Barcos*

Cover Production: *Russell Leong Design*

Book Design & Production: *London Road Design*

Printer: *Bawden Printing*

**Library of Congress Card Catalog Number 89-081244**

**ISBN 1-56052-484-7**

*My sincerest thanks and appreciation to Mike Denton*
*for his invaluable technical assistance,*
*acting as a sounding board and for his objective feedback.*

# CONTENTS

# CONTENTS

# I.

# VALUE MANAGEMENT OVERVIEW

V ALUE MANAGEMENT (VM) is more than a tool
or technique for reducing product cost. Over
the last fifty plus years of its existence, VM has
matured into a methodology that employs a set of disciplines proven to solve a broad range of management issues
successfully and dramatically to create competitive advantage for the company. To gain some appreciation for the
scope and effectiveness of this methodology, this book
explores some key elements that make VM work so well.

English is the only Western language that uses the
two words "value" and "worth" interchangeably. *Webster's
New Collegiate Dictionary* defines "value" and "worth" as
follows:

> **Value**–a fair return or equivalent in goods or
> services or money for something exchanged: the
> *monetary worth* of something.

> **Worth**–*monetary value:* the value of something mea-
> sured by its qualities or by the esteem in which it
> is held.

In Value Management (VM), value is a marketing term.[1] It is the price assigned to goods or services at a level to attract customers and profit from their sale. Worth is a more personalized term. It expresses the buyer's view of the price as it relates to the benefits–the functions and attributes of the product or service offered. When worth equals price it's a buy situation. The word "bargain" is not considered a value term. A bargain is defined as "something you don't need at a price you can't resist."

Many value practitioners define worth as "the lowest cost to perform basic functions reliably." They use this figure to set target cost objectives for the value project. However, this does not consider the market's influences in making the sale. In VM, the marketplace exerts a major influence because it is the buyer, not the seller, who determines the value/worth relationship of a product.

In VM, the phrases "improving value" and "increasing the value-added contribution" refer to improvements in the product or service that increase the buyer's sense of its worth, as well as reduce production cost.

## In the Beginning

The search for improved value that evolved into VM began during World War II. General Electric (GE), concerned with the difficulty of obtaining critical listed materials to produce war equipment, assigned electrical engineer Lawrence D. Miles to the purchasing department. His mission was to find adequate material and component substitutes to manufacture war equipment. In his search, Miles found that each material has unique properties that could enhance the product if he modified the design to take advantage of those properties. He also discovered that he could meet or improve product performance and reduce production cost by understanding and addressing the intended function of the product. Miles separated function or the intent of the design expressed as "what it must do," from the characteristics of the design or "how it does it."[2]

As the search for cost reduction by analyzing functions grew into a procedure, Miles named the process Value Analysis. It soon evolved into a team activity directed at reducing high product and component costs while protecting the principal or "basic" functions of the product.

In 1945, the potential results of Value Analysis attracted the U.S. Navy's Bureau of Ships. It commissioned Miles to train its personnel in the process. The Bureau did not have a Value Analysis slot in its organizational table, but there were openings in the table of organization for engineers. To give organizational recognition to this effective process, the Navy renamed it Value Engineering. Today, this renaming causes a level of confusion.

Because industry and the Department of Defense use both names, definitions emerged in an attempt to justify both terms, which only led to more confusion.

The Department of Defense described Value Engineering as a "before the fact" activity, applying the value process during the product design phase. They defined Value Analysis as an "after the fact" activity, applying the value process after design release, during production.

In marketing, Value Analysis describes the search to identify product functions or attributes that have high customer value appeal. Value Engineering is the process of putting those highly valued attributes into the products being designed.

## Later Development

Following the close of WWII, the United States' manufacturing sector turned to the design and production of consumer products. Miles applied the lessons he learned during wartime to create competitively produced consumer products for GE.

Focusing on function as the way to improve value, he expressed value in the following relationship:

$$\text{Value} = \frac{\text{Function}}{\text{Cost}}$$

This relationship is the cornerstone of VM. Although expressed simply, the relationship of function to cost has broad implications.

The principal value elements used in VM studies are classified as:

- Esteem Value = Want

- Exchange Value = Worth

- Utility Value = Need

Each decision to acquire goods or services includes one or a combination of all the value elements, where the sum of the elements results in a buy decision.

Esteem value or "want" invokes the buyer's desire to own for the sake of ownership. Collectibles fall into this category. The perception and reputation of the company can carry a quantifiable level of esteem value. Well-known companies that earned the reputation for–or are perceived as–producing high-quality products, support and innovation can command a higher price for essentially the same product produced by lesser-known companies.

Exchange value or "worth" describes the buyer's perception, not the seller's. Improving an offering's worth requires a good understanding of why the product interests the buyer and how and when the buyer will use the product. These attributes can then be designed into the product.

Utility value or "need" is the primary value element the design engineer must address. Utility describes the performance and physical characteristics of the product, usually measured in engineering terms.

VM defines *function* as the intent or purpose of a system, product or process operating in its normally prescribed manner. Using these defined value terms expands the previous equation into the following value relationship:

$$\text{Value} = \frac{(\text{Esteem})(\text{Exchange})(\text{Utility})}{\text{Cost}}$$

Figure 1 illustrates the dynamics of this value expression, and indicates value improvement paths. As shown in Figure 1, value can be increased by favorably influencing function and/or cost. In the upper row, three of the four examples show that improving the function can improve

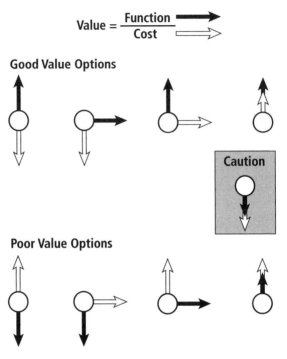

*Figure 1.    Function/Cost relationship*

value. This is true only if the customer is willing to pay for the improved functions. Improving functions without increasing perceived buyer value, or worth, will not increase sales or market value.

The center symbol, labeled Caution, identifies an opportunity to improve value by reducing or eliminating secondary functions that are cost-drivers. However, the value practitioner should not disturb those customer-sensitive functions that are the primary reason for the product's success. Customer-sensitive functions are not always obvious, so the value practitioner should use caution and check with market sources before deciding on this course of action.

Price can determine market value, when all else is equal. The daily flower auction in Aalsmeer, Netherlands, is an example. The process is called a Dutch Auction. Buyers view flowers in lot quantities and the seller establishes a starting price. Every few seconds a large clock lowers the price until a buyer electronically signals a "buy." The process continues until buyers purchase all the flowers. In this example, the buyer truly establishes the market value of the product.

## Value Management

Value analysis and value engineering describe the use of the process, but do not define the terms. This book offers a third term, Value Management, to describe the value process:

> **Value Management.** Value Management is an organized effort directed at analyzing the functions of goods and services to achieve those necessary functions and essential characteristics in the most profitable manner.

The following comments explain the key elements of this definition.

***An Organized Effort.*** VM is a structured building block process that consists of defined steps called the "job plan."

*Analyzing and Achieving Necessary Functions.* VM makes a deliberate effort to identify what the market furnishes and what it needs, as opposed to the supplier's perception of wants. The process interfaces engineering and marketing to define the priority requirements from the point of view of the customer and includes the target price and life cycle cost.

*Essential Characteristics.* In addition to achieving the basic functions of the product or process, the product or process must also satisfy other requirements and attributes such as quality, time to market, safety, maintainability, etc.

*In the Most Profitable Manner.* VM methods determine cost generation and evaluate a range of alternatives including new concepts, reconfiguration, eliminating or combining items, and process or procedure changes. Evaluation considers the operation and maintenance of the product over its normal life expectancy—the cost of ownership.

These elements interface marketing, engineering and manufacturing. How then do the terms Value Engineering and Value Analysis fit in? VM is a methodology. Value Engineering and Value Analysis describe the application of this methodology.

**Value Engineering.** Deals with problems or opportunities involving the physical sciences as the principle discipline in its resolution (product oriented)

**Value Analysis.** Deals with problems or opportunities involving management, administrative systems analysis and processes as the principle disciplines in its resolution (people oriented)

Another term associated with VM is "Value Criteria." This term describes the efforts within a company to establish performance standards for maintaining the VM activities.

Value Criteria established professional standards and approaches for governing the effective application of the value disciplines. Some Value Criteria are:

- Policies and procedures

- Standards of performance

- Education and training

- Texts and training aids

- System performance audits

Figure 2 illustrates the relationship of these terms.

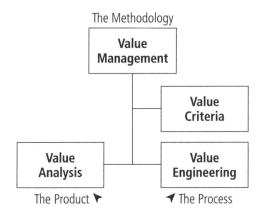

*Figure 2.*   *Value management components*

Value Management is a versatile methodology. This versatility is its strength, but also its weakness. Its strength is that VM can be molded to accommodate any market area, company, culture, organizational structure or study area. Companies use the Value Criteria to customize VM, adapting its methodology to fit a particular industry's characteristics. Its weakness is that VM serves many areas, so does not fit comfortably into an organizational slot. VM is neither an art nor a science, although both are necessary to use this discipline effectively. As a result, VM organizational units can be found in engineering, manufacturing, procurement, finance and a variety of management areas.

## The Objective of Value Management

Simply stated, the objective of VM is to "take deliberate action to improve cost effectiveness." In this definition, the terms "deliberate action" and "cost effectiveness" require further explanation to understand VM's direction and effort.

"Deliberate action" requires education and training, planning, organizational identity and accountability. "Cost effectiveness" not only includes cost reduction, but also encompasses the efforts to avoid cost, increase sales and improve profits.

## A Changing World

When Value Analysis gained popularity in 1945, industrial management methods were much different in the

United States than they are today. Component cost reduction was an effective and popular way to improve value. Manufacturing labor was the dominant business expense factor. Companies accumulated massive amounts of labor data and analyzed, dissected, restructured and categorized labor costs. Learning curves, economy of scale and material flow were key elements in the drive to reduce labor's contribution to product cost. Direct labor and material cost management determined the success of a product and, therefore, the company.

The rapid developments in communications and manufacturing technology changed the manufacturing environment. In today's world, bigger is not necessarily better. Compared to the manufacturing environment 30 to 40 years ago, direct labor and material expenses occupy a much smaller part of total product cost, and continue to shrink. Economy of scale has given way to flexible manufacturing techniques where lot sizes and set-up expense are no longer a major cost issue. Time to market, from innovative product development to market entry, has taken on more importance in business success than unit product cost.

The focus of VM has shifted from unit product cost to the production process. This is not to say that reducing direct product cost is not important. Product cost reduction is still an active VM target, but reducing the cost of doing business and associated non-value-adding activities is taking on greater emphasis.

Since its inception, VM has expanded into many market sectors and is recognized throughout the world.

VM, and its subsets Value Engineering and Value Analysis, are widely used in many industries, including automotive, aerospace, construction, petroleum, chemicals, process control, food, construction, defense, communications, consumer products, services, health care and government. The United States, Japan, South Korea, China, England, France, Germany, Hungary, Russia, Australia, Italy and India are but a few of the countries that have organized VM associations. The European Economic Community has made Value Management a standing committee, supporting VM congresses in member countries every other year.

## Applications

The application of VM is diverse. As a methodology, companies have used VM for new product development, project and business planning, business system re-engineering, technical and management process development, and a variety of projects classified as "problem solving."

### *The Problem with Problem Solving*

The Value Management process begins with identifying a problem or an opportunity that needs resolution. Many problem-solving approaches and variations are available. The problem with most problem-solving disciplines, however, is that they assume that the stated problem is the real problem. Furthermore, problems are usually expressed as symptoms or the effects of the problem that is bothering the problem definer. Problems defined in this manner usually result in a solution to the symptoms instead of the problem. And the root problem can emerge in another form, often with greater magnitude than the original problem.

## Defining the Problem

Peter Drucker, noted author, business analyst, professor, and management authority, once said that he would "much prefer to arrive at the wrong solution to the right problem than find the right solution for the wrong problem." And John Dewey's observation that "a problem well-defined is half-solved" stresses the need to invest the time to uncover the root cause of the problem.

Defining root cause problems for interdisciplinary teams to resolve is particularly important in the VM process. Each team member will interpret the information to fit his or her own expertise. The engineer will modify the description of the problem to comfortably fit his discipline, as will the finance, quality, manufacturing, and other team members.

Another dilemma is that managers who have trouble articulating the root problem will often describe it as cost-related. "Cost reduction" they say, "is our biggest problem and we must take all steps to aggressively reduce cost." But cost reduction is *not* a problem; it is a *solution* to a problem. Very often managers can trace the need for cost reduction to real problems such as declining sales, profit improvement, eroding market share, time to market, new product introduction, competitive pressures or return on assets. The effective use of VM requires that the team clearly understand the target problem so that they can focus cost reduction on that problem. Consider also that cost reduction may contribute to the resolution of that problem, but by itself, the best option may not include cost reduction.

Value practitioners fully appreciate that the success of products and services in the marketplace depends on offering functions for which the market is willing to pay. The value practitioner also realizes that those functions are not readily apparent. To attack cost aggressively without knowing which functions and attributes are "customer-sensitive" could result in dramatic cost reductions, but those actions could also adversely affect sales.

## Some Examples

A seemingly successful VM cost-reduction project to reduce the unit cost (and price) of a line of thermocouples did nothing to reverse the downward trend in sales and market share. A follow-up project analysis found the root problem was not the price charged for the product, but the time it took to respond to an order. A second VM project focused on improving the order entry process and reducing the time from receipt of an order to its delivery. The resultant reduction in order response time, from two weeks to three days, achieved the sales recovery objective.

In the public sector, the city of New York employed VM to reduce the eight-plus years it took to refurbish and modernize high schools. Before beginning the process the team discussed the problem in terms of seeking time-saving measures. When the problem was better defined, the team determined that the eight-year restoration was a symptom, not the problem. They discovered that the real problem was that no individual or department took responsibility for the complete project. There was no single point of responsibility or accountability for the "turn key" management of a high school refurbishment project. Therefore, each participating department considered their part of the project a low-priority activity. The VM team focused on the organizational issues and created a project-management structure. The result, supported by a follow-up audit, reduced the restoration time by more then half.

Many other examples emphasize the need to uncover the "real" problem before seeking a solution. Miles expressed this search in a list of five questions.

1.  What is it?

2.  What does it do?

3.  What does it cost?

4.  What else will do the job?

5.  What does that cost?

These simple questions, asked and answered in sequence, led to the development of a process called the Job Plan.

# II.

# THE JOB PLAN

---

T HE JOB PLAN is key to the VM methodology. This is a disciplined approach consisting of sequenced steps that guide the VM team through the problem (or opportunity) solving process. Miles developed the original five-step job plan, still used today. Although users can modify the plan to fit their Value Criteria requirements, the original form is part of every VM workshop.

## Five Steps

All forms of the job plan include the following five steps:

**Step 1: Information**–Evaluation of all available information relation to the VM project and translation of that information into function terms.

**Step 2: Speculation**–Process of developing a large quantity of ideas (not solutions) that address unique and creative ways to achieve those functions that relate to the problem definition.

**Step 3: Planning (or Analysis)**–Evaluation of the ideas previously generated, using weighted guidelines, performance, and other requirements, to sift and sort for the "best" ideas.

**Step 4: Execution (or Evaluation)**–Clustering of selected ideas into proposal scenarios and the evaluation of those scenarios that include financial, risk and implementation plan recommendations.

**Step 5: Reporting (or Presentation)**– Preparation and presentation of recommended VM Team proposals to a management board (or stakeholders), seeking approval and funding to implement those actions to resolve the problem or opportunity objectives.

The discipline associated with the Job Plan is in following the steps in sequence. This is a building block process in which it is often necessary to repeat a step or two, but the value practitioner must never skip any steps (see Figure 3).

Figure 4 illustrates the thinking process behind the five steps of the Job Plan. Divergent (or right-brain) thinking explores the unique by stimulating and applying the

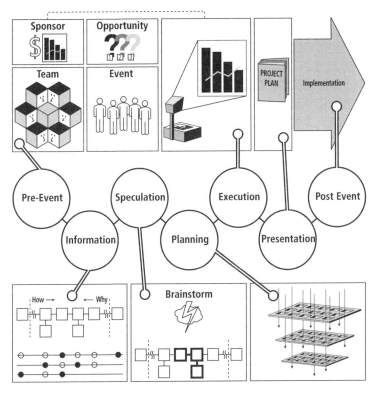

*Figure 3.  Job Plan steps*

VM team's creative traits. Convergent (or left-brain) thinking explores relevancy, applying the principals of logic and quantitative analysis techniques. The Information and Speculation phases require divergent thinking, while Planning, Execution and Presentation require convergent thinking.

The search to uncover the root cause problem is considered a divergent thinking process because it requires

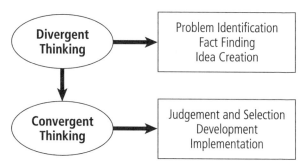

*Figure 4.    Value management thinking process*

creativity to separate symptoms from root problems, and adequately define the problem in a way that leads to a solution.

## The Pre-Event Phase

As the VM methodology progressed from reducing the cost of components to more complex issues, a "pre-event" step was added to the Job Plan process to address and sort through a greater volume of information and complex issues. The activities within the Pre-Event Phase describe the planning and resolution of issues that must be achieved prior to the start of the VM Task Team's efforts to resolve the project's objectives. The Pre-Event Phase is considered an extension of the Job Plan's Information Phase.

The Implementation Phase is a critical part of the VM process, but implementation is a post VM workshop activity. Although the Pre-Event and Post Event Phases are part of the VM Job Plan, they sandwich the VM workshop where the Job Plan occurs. During the Pre-Event

Phase an Executive Review Board (ERB) is formed consisting of those managers representing the internal customers, or stakeholders. It is the ERB that receives and approves the VM team's proposals and authorizes the resources necessary to implement the proposal's recommendations.

To begin the process, the VM Task Team facilitator(s) hold a Pre-Event meeting with the sponsor or stakeholders (Executive Review Board) and key team members. The Pre-Event Phase encompasses a series of steps to define, confirm and plan the project. Pre-event activities help the team acquire and process information in a dependent sequence. The activities described in the gathering of information during the Pre-event phase help the team test the information received and resolve any conflicting information.

To those learning the process, VM appears to spend an inordinate amount of time gathering and analyzing data before and during the project resolution process. The following rule explains a reason for this:

> *The quality of decisions cannot consistently rise above the quality of information upon which those decisions are made.*

A corollary to this rule is:

> *Considering time constraints, there is never enough time available to make a "no risk" decision.*

Although arriving at a no risk problem solution is a virtual impossibility, the VM process identifies and evaluates technical and economic risk in arriving at proposal recommendations. A benefit-risk analysis will then determine the wisdom of the resolution investment.

## *Exploring Pre-Event Techniques*

Pre-event work includes the activities listed in Figure 5. Each of the activities described has a technique or tool associated with that activity.

***3 Questions.*** The VM project starts with a desire to correct a problem or capture an opportunity. Usually, the project assignment is given to an individual or team who plans the direction and actions of the project, then acts to implement that plan to solve the problem. Inherent in the VM process is the need to confirm that the problem described is the "right" problem. A problem statement

| Activities | Techniques |
|---|---|
| 1. Define the problem (or opportunity), separating cause from effect. | 3 Questions |
| 2. Establish goals that, if accomplished, will resolve the problem. | Goals and Objectives |
| 3. Define attributes that identify market-driving value-adding characteristics. | Starmodel or Rank and Rate |
| 4. Identify perceptions that stand in the way of achieving the goals. | Roadblocks |
| 5. Determine the disciplines needed to explore creative alternatives. | Creating Teams |
| 6. Collect information by disciplines that relate to the problem issues. | Project Information |

*Figure 5.    Pre-event steps*

is then developed that will guide the team in seeking resolutions.

The questions asked to discover the problem may seem simple, but often require intense discussion among the project sponsors and the VM team to arrive at an acceptable answer. The questions are:

1. What is the problem (or opportunity) we are about to resolve?

2. Why do you believe this is a problem?

3. Why is a solution necessary? (or what is the consequence of not solving the problem?)

If the answer to the first question answers the second, the problem as described is an imposed solution, symptom or effect of the real problem, rather than the root cause.

For example, when asked what problem the sponsor wished resolved, the answer was "Cost. The cost of our 'super widget' is too high which is adversely effecting the sales of our entire line of widgets." This answer fits the second question. So the team facilitator then asked the problem owner why the cost of widgets is considered a problem, considering that there was no appreciable increase in widget cost over the last few years. The sponsor answered, "Our competitor has lowered its price which has resulted in lost sales, market share and profit for us."

On examination, the problem owner's response to why cost was a problem identified the root problem as lost sales due to competitive price pressures. With this new information, the sponsor and team agreed to the answers to the three questions.

1.  What is the problem (or opportunity) we are about to resolve?

    *Our competitor has recently reduced the price of the product offering that competes with our widget product line.*

2.  Why do you believe this is a problem?

    *The price reduction has resulted in lost sales and revenue in our widget line. If we respond by reducing our price to meet the competition, without reducing cost, it will result in lost profits.*

3.  Why is a solution necessary?

    *If we do not recover the loss of sales and revenue of our widget product line, it will adversely affect the profit objectives of our business plan, which could affect growth.*

By restating the problem conditions, the problem was redefined as competitive pressures, not cost reduction. Cost reduction is not a problem condition, it is a recommended solution to the problem. Reducing the cost of the widgets seemed like the obvious approach, but better approaches may exist. Searching for ways to improve competition offers a much broader range of study than only seeking cost-reduction opportunities. Some avenues to explore are: thinning out the losing end of widget models, enhancing value-adding product features and attri-butes (such as performance, quality, service, delivery, etc.), improving product yield, increasing inventory turns, and other nondirect expense areas.

The resulting VM actions may not need to match the competitors' price reduction. Improving value-adding features can justify and support higher prices if customers perceive those improvements as worth the price difference.

***Goals and Objectives.*** With the resolution of the problem statement, the team established the goals and objectives based on the root problem. The team can now consider the business and product performance goals. Business goals focus on the direct and indirect expense areas that will reduce product cost. A comparison of widget features and attributes with its competitor's product may expose competitor weaknesses and widget strengths that the team could study for value-adding proposal candidates.

Wherever possible, the team should set aggressive and quantitative goals. Once the sponsors brief the VM team, the sponsors should allow the task team to set its own project goals. Experience shows that goals the team sets for itself are more challenging than those set by the sponsor or the Executive Review Board.

The terms "optimize"or "maximize" are meaningless in setting team goals and should be avoided. To optimize widget performance or maximize the widget's cost-to-price ratio does not offer a clear target for the team. The terms are subject to wide interpretation by the team members and project sponsors.

Some goals are difficult to express in quantitative terms. Attributes such as "ease of use" and "customer satisfaction" are hard to measure, but valid as value-adding characteristics.

***Star Model or Rank and Rate.*** With goals in place, the team selects the project attributes that support the project goals. These are then evaluated, graded and graphically illustrated in a star diagram. The star diagram guides the team in determining where the company can trade lower-value attributes for higher-value attributes. (See Chapter 5 for a discussion of star diagrams.)

The selected attributes are prioritized and graded using a paired-comparison process. Grading the attributes ranks them in descending order of importance by determining a percentage grade for each attribute. The total grade value of all the attributes will always equal 100. With the attributes weighted, the team can explore ways of trading lesser value attributes for those of higher value during the Speculation and Planning phases of the Job Plan.

A minimum of five and maximum of eight attributes are recommended for each team project. Exceeding eight attributes creates a difficult balancing act in determining trade-off options. Fewer then five attributes could place too large of a weight difference between attributes that could place undue importance on a selected proposal path.

Certainly "product cost" is an important attribute in our simple widget example. How important depends on an investigation of the project issues,other goal-related attributes and their relationship to achieving the primary objective of competitive advantage. Other attributes, selected from a wide variety of options in addition to product cost, include: quality, performance, weight, after-market support, maintainability, ease of use, delivery and others. (Chapter 3 discusses how to define and measure each attribute.)

***Roadblocks.*** With a better understanding of the project goals and issues to be resolved, the pre-event participants discuss and list roadblocks. Roadblocks, or sacred cows, are non-functional constraints, perceived restrictions or paradigms that stand in the way of achieving the project objectives.

The key word in the definition is "perceived." If the participant perceives that a restriction exists, the participant's actions and decisions will treat and reflect that restriction as fact. A second important term is "non-functional." Roadblocks do not relate directly to the functional requirements. Most roadblocks emerge from tradition, policies or regulations.

By discussing and listing the roadblocks, they can be confirmed or discarded by the project owner or ERB representative. Those that remain are set aside to be re-evaluated against solution options. If a roadblock conflicts with a proposed solution, the team determines its origin and studies ways of overcoming that concern or constraint.

Roadblocks originate to prevent the recurrence of an unwanted condition, but that condition is rarely described. To determine the origin of the roadblock, ask, "What problem or unwanted condition will we avoid by complying with the constraint?" After determining and understanding the concerns, consider: "Is there a better way?"

Some examples of roadblocks randomly selected from a variety of VM studies follow. The (I) refers to internal roadblocks, (E) to external roadblocks. Most roadblock lists will show that the majority of constraints are internally generated, rather then imposed by external sources.

- Contracts will always be awarded to the lowest bidder. (I)

- Stainless steel is the only acceptable material. (I)(E)

- Products must be sized to fit standard shipping containers. (I)

- Printed circuit boards can only be purchased from our sister division. (I)

- It is better to please the boss then satisfy the customers. (I)

- Butt weld joints are unacceptable. (I)(E)

- The product must meet all environmental specifications. (E)

***VM Teams.*** At this point in the pre-event process, the participants should form an idea of the number of teams and the disciplines needed in the teams to resolve the project issues.

VM teams are interdisciplinary. Why an interdisciplinary team? Many years ago, an analyst facilitated a Value Engineering team study in the chemical industry. The team consisted of eight chemical engineers. It is not surprising that only chemical solutions were considered.

A reason to form teams of like-disciplined people is because common interests work well together. Team members can communicate with each other and objectively and professionally gauge other team members' contributions. However, they lack a sympathetic concern for the impact their decisions have on other areas in the organization. Unfortunately, homogeneous or single-disciplined teams often create more problems by their resolutions than they solve.

## *Selecting Team Members*

Three questions govern which disciplines should be represented on the team. These are:

1. Who owns the problem?

2. Who is responsible for the resolution of the problem?

3. Who will be impacted by the resolution?

Answering the first question, the person or unit most affected by the problem should be represented on the team. This is to ensure that in addressing the problem owner's or stakeholder's problem, the focus is on the correct problem, not its symptoms.

Answering the second question is easier if the problem to be resolved is correctly defined. That problem definition will suggest which disciplines should be involved in resolving it. Those disciplines will also be responsible for implementing the proposed resolutions. If the problem is management-driven, then managers should serve on the team. If the problem is technical, then the technical staff should be represented.

The third question is important because it further ensures that the problem, not its symptoms, will be addressed. Including representatives for areas potentially affected by the proposed resolutions will also ensure that the solution to the defined problem does not create greater problems in other areas.

Referring to our widget example, a two sub-team workshop is a consideration. One team would address cost-reduction opportunities while the second team focuses on improving value-adding attributes. The teams would conduct their studies concurrently, coming together as a single team at the planning phase of the Job Plan to form joint proposals.

Some disciplines to consider in forming the teams include marketing, manufacturing engineering, design engineering (electrical, mechanical, systems, etc.), industrial design, cost estimating, quality, procurement and finance (or cost accounting). Also, depending on the direction and structure of the workshop, the team make-up should include a customer or distributor representative, suppliers and a "wild card." A wild card is an individual who is competent in discussing the project issues, but who does not have a vested interest in the study and is therefore considered unbiased. Wild cards are selected from other projects, divisions, companies or industries to break through paradigm constraints.

The core or full-time team should range from five to eight participants. Other services can be added to the team on an as-needed or part-time basis, but the core team should be small, relevant and focused on the project.

***Project Information.*** With the project team(s) named, the team participants are given information-gathering assignments of specific and general information, by discipline, needed for the VM process. Team members will search their data resources to gather and compile the information into a project data bank.

Each problem and project has unique conditions that requires a case-specific information checklist. This checklist should be developed during the Pre-Event Phase.

## Widget Project Checklist

Here is the checklist for our widget project.

### *From Marketing and Sales*

- Markets served by the product, displayed in a pie chart of both percent and dollars

- Product price necessary to achieve market goal

- Competitor's specifications, costs, and product example (if possible)

- Market analysis of valued attributes

- Customer suggestions on features to add or delete

- Competitor's strengths and weaknesses

- Delivery and distribution effectiveness

- Image, service appraisal

### *From Manufacturing*

- Restrictive tolerances of dimensions

- Expensive design specifications

- High scrap and rework areas
- Current and future capital equipment needs
- Work in process, process flow
- Our production cost vs. competition (estimate)
- Make or buy considerations
- Bottlenecks in the manufacturing process

### *From Engineering*

- Restrictive product performance specifications
- Unusual environmental or operational requirements
- Pet ideas worth exploring
- Detailed drawings, concepts, sketches, models, photos and hardware
- Technical advances that may apply
- New material advances
- New product ideas

### *From Purchasing*

- ABC material cost break-out
- Single or sole source–why?
- High-cost engineering requirements
- High-cost receiving inspection–rejection
- Suppliers suggestions for cost reduction

### *From Quality Assurance/Field Support*

- Design features not used or infrequently used
- Recurring customer complaints and compliments
- Field service problems
- Suggested areas for redesign
- Service failure trends

### *From Finance/Cost Accounting*

- Product cost break-out (standard product cost plus overhead support accounts)
- High cost drivers
- High-cost shop areas
- High-variance cost areas
- Major rework cost centers
- Trend analysis, cost-to-price ratios

### *From General Management*

- Business cycles
- Group management policies, direction
- Facility and capital plans
- "Partnering" or "alliance" agreements
- Investment constraints

# III.

## FUNCTION ANALYSIS

T HE VALUE MANAGEMENT PROCESS starts with the information phase, usually in the form of an off-site workshop. In the opening session, team members report on the results of their information-gathering efforts. They adjust problem statement, project goals, roadblocks and attributes as necessary based on the information presented and discussed. With this part of the VM process resolved, the team develops a *function model* or diagram that graphically illustrates the problem. The Function Analysis System Technique (FAST), discussed in detail in Chapter 4, provides a useful model.

As stated in Chapter 1, *function* is the end result desired by the customer; it is what the customer pays for. It is the goal, not an action. But it is the result of an action.

*Function analysis* is the cornerstone of the VM methodology. It is the one discipline that separates VM from the many problem-solving initiatives and processes available.

# Describing Functions

The discovery of the power of function analysis is credited to the creative imagination of Lawrence D. Miles. Function analysis separates the intent or purpose of something from its description, then improves its value by manipulating its functions.

Miles used a verb-noun discipline to express functions, prescribing an *active* verb and a *measurable* noun in combination.

Some examples of describing functions are:

- A spring does not move parts, it "stores energy."

- A screwdriver does not turn screws, it "transmits torque."

- An oil filter does not clean oil, it "traps particles."

## *Active Verbs*

When identifying the functions of components, products or processes, it is important to use active, rather than passive, verbs. The verb describes the action and the noun defines the object of that action. Searching for the most descriptive verb-noun combination is difficult. Compromise often results in selecting the action as the noun and using a passive verb to complete the function description. If you suspect a passive description of a function or you wish to express the function more actively, try to use the noun as a verb and then select another noun.

For example:

| Passive | Active |
|---------|--------|
| Provide *support* | *Support* weight |
| Seek *approval* | *Approve* budget |
| Develop *exhibits* | *Exhibit* products |
| Submit *budget* | *Budget* expenses |
| Determine *resolution* | *Resolve problem* |

Functions are intended to be taken literally. Avoid the verbs "provide," "review," "attend," and verbs ending in "ize."

"Provide" is often used when the function is not understood.

"Review," as in "review proposals," means read or skim but do not comment or take further action. If this is the intent of the function, then the function is correctly stated. But if you want someone to respond to the proposals, you must say so: "evaluate proposals" or "correct proposals."

"Attend" means different things depending on where it is used. For a staff member to "attend meetings" means that the person is just expected to sit there. But for a nurse to "attend patient" means that the nurse is expected to care for the patient.

Using "ize," such as "prioritize," "modernize," and "economize," is shorthand for a description of activities and should not be avoided in describing functions.

## *Measurable Nouns*

Measurable nouns are easier to determine when the study topic is a hardware example. When hardware components are used, measurements are quantitative and often expressed as engineering units. Examples of measurable nouns include: weight, force, load, heat, light, radiation, current, flow and energy. Functions such as "control flow," "reduce weight" and "transmit torque" have nouns that can be universally measured. In hardware systems, functions such as "repair damage," "complete circuit" and "store parts" have nouns that can be quantitatively measured, but do not easily fit conventionally measurable nouns. "Damage" can be measured in terms of cost or time to repair; "circuit" can be measured by the size of the network or energy consumed; "parts" can be measured by quantity or dimensions.

Selecting the appropriate measurement for hardware systems depends on the problem to be resolved. In non-hardware applications, such as business processes, functions like "transfer responsibility," "create proposal" and "develop plan" can be measured in terms of time, people or "softer" measurement units. Again, the problem to be resolved will determine what measurements to use. Using measurable nouns to describe functions is important for evaluating and selecting the best proposal alternatives to resolve the problem, and for presenting the proposals for approval and funding authorization.

Many sell functions such as "improve appearance," "establish prestige" and "enhance features" are considered secondary, but they are important if they contribute to the sale of the product. After all, the objective is to improve value as determined by the buyer, not simply to reduce cost.

## *Using Two Words to Describe Functions*

Using two-word function descriptions in problem solving is essential because it cuts through technical jargon. These descriptions create a communication format that allows members of an interdisciplinary team to communicate with each other. It allows scientists to communicate with financial analysts, engineers with procurement, and manufacturing with marketing. To cite an example, if the finance representative on our hypothetical interdisciplinary team presented an idea for consideration, the person might say:

> Give consideration to obtaining our product at the present time while deferring actual expenditures of capital to a future period.

In time, after some questioning, the suggestion would be understood. But using the verb-noun approach, this idea could be expressed as: buy now, pay later.

Although the many subtleties of finance might not be immediately apparent, the team better understands and can agree on what is being suggested.

Using two words, an active verb and measurable noun, may sound like a simple procedure, but it is not in fact an easy thing to do. Miles recognized the difficulty, and sometimes frustration, in trying to find those two words that could most accurately describe the function of the item under study. The team must then confirm understanding by arriving at consensus on the function description. In his book *Techniques of Value Analysis,* Miles said, "While the naming of functions may appear simple, the exact opposite is true. In fact, naming them articulately is so difficult and requires such precision in thinking that real care must be taken to prevent abandonment of the task before it is accomplished."

## Defining and Classifying Functions

The word "function" is commonly used and has many definitions. For our purpose, a function is defined as "an intent or purpose that a product or service is expected to perform."

The two operative words in this definition are "intent" and "expected." How a product or service is used does not identify its functions. A book may make an excellent doorstop, but the function of a book is not to "prevent movement."

In developing the value methodology, Miles classified and defined functions to assist in separating them from their design descriptions. Once defined, functions can be examined and analyzed to determine their contribution to the value equation:

$$\text{Value} = \frac{\text{Function}}{\text{Cost}}$$

The classifications of functions as they relate to product performance are:

**Basic Function:** The principal reason(s) for the existence of the product or service, operating in its normally prescribed manner.

**Secondary Function:** The method(s) selected to carry out the basic function(s) or those functions and features supporting the basic functions.

Many value practitioners prefer a simplified definition that describes a basic function as "anything that makes the product work or sell," with all other functions categorized as "secondary" functions.

Secondary functions are sometimes sub-classified as "required" functions. This describes a function or feature that may not contribute to a basic function but is mandated by a customer as a condition to a sale. The size and layout of a personal computer keyboard, the emergency brake in an automobile and the buttons on the sleeves of men's sport jackets all represent costly features or functions that do not contribute directly to the product's basic function, but are mandated by the customer. Eliminating or modifying those secondary function items would not affect, and may enhance, the product's performance. However, not satisfying these requirements could result in lost sales.

## Rules Governing Basic Functions

Four rules, or characteristics, determine which are the basic functions. These four are important in selecting functions and classifying them as basic:

1. Once defined, a basic function cannot change.

2. The cost to satisfy a basic function is usually less than 5 percent of the total product cost.

3. You cannot sell basic functions alone, but the supporting (secondary) functions cannot be sold without first satisfying the basic function.

4. The loss of the basic function(s) causes the loss of the market value and worth of the product or service.

***Rule 1: Once defined, a basic function cannot change.***
Those functions designated as basic represent the operative functions of the item or product, and must be maintained and protected. Determining the basic function of single components can be relatively simple. The basic function of a spring is to "store energy," a screwdriver "transmits torque," a filter "traps particles."

As components form to become assemblies and assemblies combine to create products, determining the basic function becomes more complex. Is the basic function of a butane lighter to "create heat" or "produce flame?" The answer depends on the problem or issues to be resolved. If the company that is designing a new butane lighter also has economic ties to the production of lighter fuel, then "produce flame" would be the obvious choice. However, if the designers are a new venture company without product constraints, the basic function would be "create heat," because "create heat" gives the designers more creative freedom in designing their product than "produce flame."

The same rationale holds in identifying the basic function of a pencil. Is the basic function of a pencil to "make marks" or "deposit graphite?" To "make marks" offers more creative paths to explore than "deposit graphite," but you must first determine the problem to be resolved before selecting the basic function.

By definition, functions designated as "basic" will not change, but the way those functions are implemented is open to innovation.

***Rule 2: The cost to satisfy a basic function is usually less than 5 percent of the total product cost.*** As important as the basic function is to the success of any product, the cost to perform that function is inversely proportional to its importance. This is not an absolute rule, but rather an observation of the consumer products market.

Value Management defines worth as "the lowest cost to perform that function reliably." The basic function of a one-dollar disposable lighter, "produce flame," can be reliably achieved with a match costing less than one-tenth of a cent. The basic function of a Rolex watch that costs $20,000 can be expressed as "indicate time." A no-name, blister-packed wristwatch, displayed on a self-serve rack and purchased in a drugstore for less then $20.00, can perform that function reliably. Why do people purchase Rolex watches? Certainly not for the ability or accuracy in performing the function "indicate time." People buy Rolex watches to show other people that they can afford to buy Rolex watches. Creating a perception of success by possessing a Rolex is the primary motivation for the purchase.

However, if that $20,000 watch did not work, and it could not be repaired, in terms of function loss the value of "indicate time" is $20.00 out of $20,000. Could you then say that the broken watch is worth $19,980.00? This leads us to the third rule.

**Rule 3: You cannot sell basic functions alone, but the supporting (secondary) functions cannot be sold without first satisfying the basic function.** Few people purchase consumer products based on performance or the lowest cost of basic functions alone. When purchasing a product, a customer assumes that the basic function is operative. The customer directs his or her attention to those visible secondary support functions or product features, which determine the worth of the product.

From a product design point of view, products that are perceived to have high value first address the basic functions' performance, stressing the achievement of all of the performance attributes. Once the basic functions are satisfied, the designers then address which secondary functions are necessary to distinguish the product from their competitors' products and attract customers. Secondary functions are incorporated in the product as features to support and enhance the basic function and help sell the product.

The elimination of non-customer-sensitive secondary functions will reduce product cost, increasing value without detracting from the worth of the product. Changing customer-sensitive functions will change the customer's perception of the product's value, which could have positive or negative effects on sales.

*Rule 4: The loss of the basic function(s) causes the loss of the market value and worth of the product or service.* The cost contribution of the basic function does not, by itself, establish the value of the product. Few products are sold on the basis of their basic function alone. If this were so, the market for generic brands would be larger than it is. Although the cost contribution of the basic function is relatively small, its loss, as illustrated in the lighter and watch examples, will cause the loss of the market value of the product.

## Function Examples

Figure 6 gives a number of verb and noun combinations for a common fuse. Each describes a function of the fuse. Try selecting the combination that best describes the fuse's basic function.

If you selected "break circuit," why not remove the fuse and not replace it in the circuit? How about "connect circuit?" If this is the basic function, why not eliminate the

**Find the BASIC FUNCTION of a:**

**Fuse**

| Random Functions | |
|---|---|
| **Verb** | **Noun** |
| Break | Circuit |
| Connect | Circuit |
| Protect | User |
| Protect | Supplier |
| Protect | Equipment |
| Identify | Failures |
| Advertises | Mfgr. |

*Figure 6. Fuse functions*

fuse from the circuit and connect the wire ends? Or consider "protect equipment." If this is the accepted basic function, then ideas such as a security fence, guards, and guard dogs could be considered in brainstorming the basic function "protect equipment."

Do any of the functions accurately describe the basic function? If not, can you think of one that does?

A description of the fuse would be "to protect electrical equipment by preventing electrical surges beyond the circuit tolerance, from entering the circuit and destroying components that are not rated to accept the surge current." Remembering that a function describes "what it does" rather then "why it does it," the answer would be "limit current."

## Random Function Determination

The above methods describe the function analysis technique created by Lawrence Miles. The technique is called Random Function Determination. We randomly select the items of a product, identify their functions, then determine which of those functions are basic or secondary.

### *Levels of Abstraction*

As seen in the fuse example, a simple product can have many functions. It is necessary to find its basic function(s) and to understand the relative values of its secondary functions. To examine the product in more detail, we can move to a lower level of abstraction and examine the components of a product. The fuse consists of a glass tube, a low electrical tolerance resistance strip, terminal ends, and a bonding media to assemble the product. Each component of a fuse performs many functions, and each has at least one basic function.

## Component–Function Selection

When a function analysis was conducted on a common pencil, the pencil's basic and secondary functions were determined by evaluating the components' contributions to the overall product (see Figure 7).

The function "make marks" was selected as the basic function of the pencil and that function is accomplished by the lead in the pencil. Since all of the other functions are secondary or in support of the basic function, they are candidates for elimination, consolidation or modification to reduce the cost of the product.

| Description | Function | B | S |
|---|---|---|---|
| Pencil | Make marks | X | |
| Eraser | Remove marks | | X |
| Band | Secure eraser | | X |
| | Improve appearance | | X |
| Body | Support lead | | X |
| | Transmit force | | X |
| | Accommodate grip | | X |
| | Display information | | X |
| Paint | Protect wood | | X |
| | Improve appearance | | X |
| Lead | Make marks | X | |

*Figure 7.* *Pencil functions*

The manipulation of secondary functions is accomplished by the creative efforts of the team, provided that the team does not change the basic function of the pencil. This does not mean that a sintered rod of carbon graphite (or lead) must be used to perform the basic function. It does mean that at the conclusion of the pencil study, the pencil must retain its ability to "make marks" in a manner that satisfies the customer.

In Random Function Determination, the manipulation of secondary functions is guided by reducing the cost contribution of performing those functions. The objective of VM, to improve value by reducing the cost-to-function relationship of a product, is achieved by eliminating or combining as many secondary functions as possible.

In the pencil example, if you make a longitudinal cut in the wooden body and carefully remove the lead, you can write (make marks) with the lead without benefit of any of the secondary or supporting functions. Does this represent the best value proposal for the pencil? Only if the proposal is successful in the marketplace.

## Function Cost Matrix

The Function Cost Matrix approach to performing function analysis is a graphical extension of the Random Function Determination method. The objective of this process is to draw the attention of the analysts away from the cost of components and focus their attention on the cost of the functions (see Figure 8).

The Function Cost Matrix displays the components of the product, and the cost of those components, along

| Function → / Components | Cost (in cents) | Remove Marks | | Secure Eraser | | Improve Appearance | | Make Marks | | Transmit Force | | Accomodate Grip | | Display Information | | Support Lead | | Protect Wood | |
|---|---|---|---|---|---|---|---|---|---|---|---|---|---|---|---|---|---|---|---|
| | | Percent | Cost | Percent | Cost | Percent | Cost | Percent | Cost | Percent | Cost | Percent | Cost | Percent | Cost | Percent | Cost | Percent | Cost |
| Eraser | 0.43 | 100 | 0.43 | | | | | | | | | | | | | | | | |
| Metal band | 0.25 | | | 50 | 0.13 | 25 | 0.06 | | | 25 | 0.06 | | | | | | | | |
| Lead | 1.20 | | | | | | | 70 | 0.84 | 30 | 0.36 | | | | | | | | |
| Body | 0.94 | | | | | 10 | 0.09 | | | 40 | 0.37 | 5 | 0.05 | 5 | 0.05 | 40 | 0.38 | | |
| Paint | 0.10 | | | | | 50 | 0.05 | | | | | | | | | | | 50 | 0.05 |
| **Total** | **2.92** | 15 | 0.43 | 4 | 0.13 | 6 | 0.20 | 29 | 0.84 | 27 | 0.79 | 2 | 0.05 | 2 | 0.05 | 13 | 0.38 | 2 | 0.05 |

← 56 →

***Figure 8.*** ***Function cost matrix***

the left vertical side of the graph. The top horizontal
legend contains the functions performed by those components, as determined in the Random Function Determination exercise. Each component is then examined to
determine how many functions that component performs,
and the cost contributions of those functions.

For example, the eraser cost .43 parts of a penny,
and 100 percent of that cost is dedicated to the function
"remove marks." The metal band, which costs .25 of a
penny, performs three functions: "secure eraser," "improve
appearance" and "transmit force" (when using the eraser).
A cost estimate roughly allocated the cost to perform those
functions by estimating the process and material cost of
the metal band component.

To determine the cost of the function "improve appearance," the illustration shows that the metal band, body and paint all contribute to that function. The analyst can now read the chart vertically to determine the cost contribution of performing the function "improve appearance."

At this point, it is more important to determine the relative cost impact of the functions than to attempt to determine the actual manufactured cost of those functions. Detailed cost estimates become more important after function analysis, when evaluating value-improvement proposals.

Reading across the row marked "total" will show the cost and percent contribution of the functions of the pencil. This will guide the team or analyst in deciding which functions to select for value improvement analysis. Note that in this example 56 percent of the cost is dedicated to supporting two functions, "make marks" and "transmit force."

## *Levels of Abstraction*

As you may surmise, a product or system that contains a great many more components than a pencil would be proportionately more complex. Simply put, one could not begin to imagine what a Function Cost Matrix of an automobile would look like after going through the pencil exercise.

The level of abstraction selected to perform the analysis governs the complexity of the process, not the number of components in a product. In our automobile example, a high level of abstraction could contain the major subsystems as the components under study, such as: the power train, chassis, electrical system, passenger compartment, etc. The result of the Function Cost Matrix analysis could focus the team's attention on the power train for further analysis. Moving to a lower level of abstraction, the power train could then be divided into its components (engine, transmission, drive shaft etc.) for a more detailed analysis.

Another approach to simplify the process while maintaining its validity is to select only the basic functions of the individual components for the function part of the matrix. This is a good approach for a simple product that has 20 to 30 components. Using Random Function Determination, find the applicable functions for each component of the product, classifying those functions into basic and secondary to that component. Then, using only the component's basic functions, display those functions on the Function Cost Matrix. Because the analysis will move to a higher level of abstraction during evaluation of the product, many of the component's basic functions displayed in the matrix will be secondary to the product. For example, the basic function of a door, to "control access," would be secondary to a house whose basic function is to "create habitat."

To summarize, each component has a basic function. However, that basic function may be considered secondary to the system the component supports, unless the basic function of the component is also the basic function of the system. In our fuse example, the basic function of the element is to "limit current," which is the same basic function of the fuse.

# IV.

# THE POWER OF FAST
# IN VALUE MANAGEMENT

FUNCTION ANALYSIS SYSTEM TECHNIQUE, or FAST, is a powerful analysis process created by Charles W. Bytheway.[3] Used correctly, the process permits people with different technical backgrounds to interact, communicate and resolve issues that require multi-disciplined considerations. Miles' verb–noun rule enhanced interdisciplinary communications. Bytheway's contribution was in linking the simply expressed random functions to describe complex systems.

The process gives us the ability to translate the language of multi-disciplined team members into a common language. Members can then better appreciate each others' contributions and the need for arriving at a workable solution. The team can also see beyond the symptoms of a problem and expose the root cause. If the FAST process had been available in biblical times, the tower of Babel would probably still be standing.

# How Does FAST Work?

FAST reinforces the communication stimulus created by Miles' verb–noun function definition rule. It creates a graphical model that allows accounting to work with research and development, finance with engineering, and so on, as the interdisciplinary team resolves multi-faceted problems. Using simple function expressions results in effective interdisciplinary communications. This is the main ingredient that makes management initiatives like Total Quality Management and Concurrent Engineering work. Used as a methodology, FAST will translate the goals and objectives of the management initiatives into action.

The major difference between the more conventional Random Function Determination and the FAST process is in analyzing a system as a complete unit, rather than randomly analyzing the component parts of a system.

Functions do not operate in a random fashion. A system exists because functions form dependency links with other functions, just as components form dependency links with other components to make the system work. FAST graphically displays function dependencies and creates a process to study function links while exploring options to improve systems or operations.

FAST can be used in any situation where a choice of exploring, creating and implementing new function combinations is encouraged. Since its introduction, FAST has been used worldwide in a variety of situations: from marketing to engineering to manufacturing; in new product development and cost reduction; for hardware and software; from the medical profession to state government;

for creating procedures, organization development and analysis; and for productivity improvement and training.

## Intuitive Logic

In the FAST model, function dependencies are determined by establishing how and why the function is performed. Lack of a specific and acceptable response to each question indicates the presence of valueless functions and, therefore, the presence of marginal activities. Test techniques expose such questionable activities.

- How and why do you "store energy"?

- How and why do you "transmit torque"?

- How and why do you "trap particles"?

The answers to these questions are also functions, which link to form a graphical illustration of the project under study.

FAST accelerates learning the project issues under study because the discipline of FAST requires that participants use the verb–noun language to describe the performance requirements of functions. This vocabulary, along with the focus on how and why, allows participants to assess the significant elements of the process quickly. This common language promotes an understanding of how decisions and actions affect process functions in business-process VM projects.

Modeling FAST gives those questions a directional reference. As in Figure 9, "how" is always read from left to right and "why" from right to left. These questions form the foundation of the FAST process.

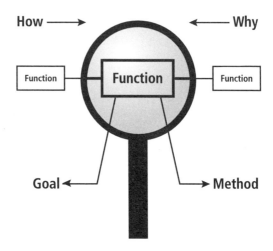

*Figure 9.  Function logic*

The importance of the how–why questions lies in the answers they invoke. When asking "how," the answer is the method to perform that function. When asking "why," the answer is the goal of that function.

Following the "how" path will lead you to a more detailed method analysis as the answers justify the functions of the subject under study. Each "how" question will bring you to a lower and more detailed level of abstraction. Asking "why" describes the systems approach and creates a higher level of abstraction. FAST requires that the team agree with the logic stream in both the "how" and "why" directions.

For example, if we are addressing the function "make marks," and asking the question, "How do we 'Make Marks'?" the answer, in the form of a function, could be "Contrast Color" (see Figure 10). We can also make marks by contrasting texture, as in making marks

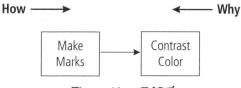

**How** ⟶                    ⟵ **Why**

*Figure 10.   FAST*

in the sand or etching, but to keep the example simple, we will not explore that logic path.

If we continue in the how direction and ask "How do we 'Contrast Color'?" one answer would be "Deposit Medium" (see Figure 11).

To test the intuitive logic of the example we can read the functions in the reverse why direction. "Why do we want to "Deposit Medium?" To "Contrast Color." Why do we want to "Contrast Color?" To "Make Marks."

If the team agrees with the answers, we can continue to expand the FAST model, either in the why or how direction. In the why direction we would ask: "Why do we want to 'Make Marks'?" To "Record Data." And "Why do we want to 'Record Data'?" To "Retrieve Information."

Returning to the how question, we can continue to build in that direction by asking, "How do we 'Deposit Medium'?" By "Applying Pressure."

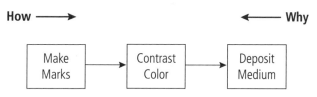

**How** ⟶                                    ⟵ **Why**

*Figure 11.   FAST logic*

Examining the function inputs thus far, the FAST model would appear as shown in Figure 12.

## Backward Thinking

The how–why orientation seems backwards to many beginners of FAST, especially those involved in creating systems diagrams or flowcharts. This is a valid observation if the principal objective is to create a systems diagram, because the why direction describes FAST in a systems orientation.

Reading the model in reverse of conventional practices is a process copy checkers use to find text errors. In our case, reading from the goal, or the left side of the model, to the beginning, on the right end, (in the how direction) goes against our system paradigm. Because it seems strange, building the model in the how–or function justification–direction, the team's attention will focus on each function element of the model. Reversing the model and building it in the system orientation (in the why direction) will cause the team to leap over individual functions and focus on the system, leaving function "gaps" in the system.

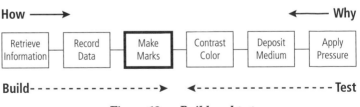

*Figure 12.   Build and test*

A good rule to remember in constructing a FAST model is to build in the how direction and test the logic in the why direction.

## The Language of FAST

The FAST language consists of five words and the symbols that define them. The five words are: *how, why, when, and* and *or*. How and why were described above and are basic to any FAST model, but using these five words to form a universal FAST language is unique to this presentation.

***Reading* When.**   The when direction is not part of the intuitive logic process, but it supplements intuitive thinking. When is not time-oriented; it expresses cause and effect. As in Figure 13, when you "Transmit Information," you should "Store Information." "Store Information" is an independent support function that supplements the function "Transmit Information." As an independent function it can be expanded in the how and why directions to build a subsystem FAST model. Because the independent function is not on the major logic path, changing or eliminating the function would not significantly affect the basic function's performances.

Always read from the exit direction of the function being addressed to question the three primary functions of how, why and when. The questions will be answered in the corresponding exit box, as shown in Figure 13.

"File Report" is an activity. Activities are not functions. They describe a specific action that is initiated

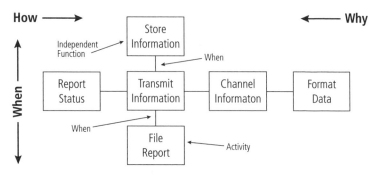

***Figure 13.*** ***Addressing HOW, WHY, WHEN***

when the logic path function is activated. Figure 13 reads "When you 'Transmit Information' you should 'File Report.'"

Because both functions and activities can be described using a verb and a noun, a general rule to distinguish between the two is to examine the noun. If the noun describes something specific like a component or device, it is considered an activity. Generic nouns describe functions. Independent functions (above the logic path) and activities (below the logic path) are the result of satisfying the when question.

Activities and functions can appear on the same logic path, as long as the how–why logic is satisfied. A FAST model that mixes activities with functions makes that model case-specific. If only functions are used to create the FAST model, it will be in generic form. As illustrated in Figure 10, the example generically expressed in function form can describe a pencil, typewriter, paint brush, printer or anything that satisfies the described how–why process to perform the basic function "Make Marks."

***Reading*** **And** *and* **Or.**   In many instances, the answer to how and why could be more than one function response. The answer could be in the form of AND or OR. The symbol for AND is a branch in the logic path and the symbol for OR is a split in the logic path showing two or more independent logic paths.

As shown in Figure 14, reading the AND branch in the HOW direction, "How do you *Confirm Compliance?* By *Verifying Documentation* AND *Validating Performance.*" Reading the OR split in the HOW direction, "How do you *Estimate Deliveries?* By Extending Bookings" OR Forecasting Orders—but not both.

## *Moving the Level of Abstraction*

Relocating activities can move the level of abstraction of the FAST model. Taking activities out of the main logic path and moving them under a related function raises the models' level of abstraction for macro analyses.

Conversely, incorporating activities into the major logic path expands and details the model, lowering the level of abstraction of the model for micro analysis.

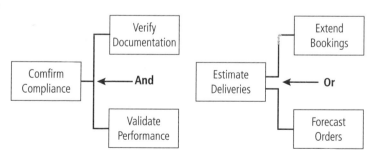

***Figure 14.***   **AND** *and* **OR**

# The Basic FAST model

The following rules and modeling characteristics are described in reference to Figure 15.

In addition to the five-word rule described above, (how, why, when, and, or), the basic FAST model contains other elements. Scope (dotted) lines indicate the scope of the project. The function to the right of the right scope line identifies the input function(s). The function(s) to the left of the left scope line identifies the higher order or objective of the project under study. The function(s) to the immediate right of the left scope line are defined as "basic" and cannot be changed. Those functions to the right of the basic function(s) are secondary or supportive. As such, they can be eliminated, modified or combined to achieve the project's goals. (See page 38 for a discussion of basic and secondary functions.)

## *Logic Paths*

Logic paths are read horizontally, or in the HOW–WHY direction. A major logic path intersects the basic function. Changes to the functions on the major logic path will significantly alter the way the basic function operates. Horizontal lines that do not intersect the basic function are minor logic paths. These functions enhance the way the basic function performs. Changes to minor logic path functions will alter the performance of the basic function but will not significantly change its selected process.

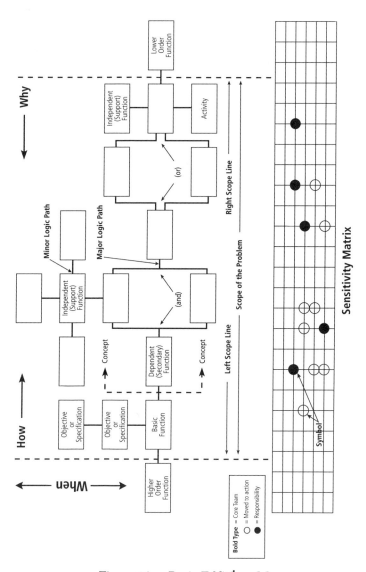

Figure 15.    Basic FAST model

## *Sensitivity Matrix*

FAST models are nondimensional. The primary purpose of a FAST model is to graphically display function dependencies. However, after completing the model it can be dimensioned in a number of ways. Using a sensitivity matrix like the one shown in Figure 15, process models can include the departments responsible or accountable for functions, activities, gates and milestone events. Other dimensions include: time between events or functions, cost per function, forms generated to satisfy functions, number of component parts to satisfy a function or groups of functions, inspection points and yield rates.

## A Case Study Using FAST

A small- to medium-sized company recently learned that its newly introduced product is an unqualified marketing success. The company needed to expand its office facilities to keep pace with the growing business. Space allocated for the production department will remain approximately the same. Management has decided to outsource detail manufacturing. The company will focus on the assembly, testing and distribution of the new product.

### *Forming the Team*

The facilities department, responsible for the management of capital assets, was requested to assess the expansion needs and ". . . do what is necessary to accommodate fully staffed sales and administrative support departments in six months or less."

The facilities manager opted to form a VM team and create a FAST model to determine what to do and identify who would be involved in implementing the assignment. The core team of full-time representatives included facilities, space planning, the occupying departments, resource planning, security, safety/fire and communications. A support team of part-time participants included marketing, procurement, personnel and information systems.

## Collecting Random Functions

Following a team management briefing that defined the problem, expectations, and constraints, the team, led by an experienced VM facilitator, randomly identified key functions associated with the assignment and displayed them in the center of a three-column chart. The purpose of randomly identifying functions is to create a "starter kit" of problem-related functions to begin constructing the FAST model. A partial example of the display appears Figure 16.

After completing the center column, the team answered the HOW and WHY questions and filled in the appropriate columns. The team tests the entry logic by reading across, in row form. For example, how do you *Define Space Requirements?* By *Analyzing Resource Needs.* And how do you *Analyze Resource Needs?* By *Forecasting Population Growth.* The logic must also hold when reading across in the WHY direction.

| ◄——— Why | Function | How ———► |
|---|---|---|
| Define space requirements | Analyize resource needs | Forecast population growth |
| (Same) | Identify growth departments | (Same) |
| Construct space Lease space Rearrange space | Allocate space | Execute plan |
| Accomodate needs | Occupy space | Implement move |
| Resolve conflicts | Identify problems | Rehearse move |
| (Other) ┊ ▼ | (Other) ┊ ▼ | (Other) ┊ ▼ |

*Figure 16.  Random function determination*

## *Constructing the FAST Model*

Each answer under the three columns is a discrete function or activity. When the team felt that it had enough functions to start the modeling process, it transcribed the functions on 1 1/2- by 2-inch Post-It notes. It then used these random notes as puzzle pieces to build the FAST model. Using the intuitive logic rules to construct the model, the random function notes are arranged in a sequential form that satisfies the HOW and WHY directions.

The functions identified are used to start the FAST model. Not all function notes will be used. Some functions may not fit the model's level of abstraction. Others may support a logic path that is not relevant to the issues. Some are discarded because they are not properly worded. Missing functions may be added to the model as needed, to bridge a logic gap in the HOW or WHY directions.

The model is considered complete when the members of the core team agree that, from their perspective, the FAST model represents the key issues of the assignment in describing *what must be done* (but not necessarily how to do it).

Figure 17 illustrates the FAST model for the facility-planning project. Although the model and its development have been simplified to fit the page-size limitations of this book, the example represents most of the elements common to all planning and process opportunities described in FAST model form. Typically, the size of a FAST model drawing will range from 11 by 17 inches to larger engineering drawing sizes. The actual model from which this example was created contains approximately four times the number of function and activity blocks shown.

## Reading and Analyzing the FAST Model

The major logic path is drawn in heavy lines. The remaining model shows activities or independent functions branching off in the WHEN direction. By definition, the first function(s) to the right of the left scope line is basic. Therefore, *Implement Move* is the basic function of the project. Reading in the HOW direction, three choices are given to implement the move. How do you *Implement Move?* By *Constructing Space* OR by *Leasing Space* OR by *Rearranging Space* or any combination of choices.

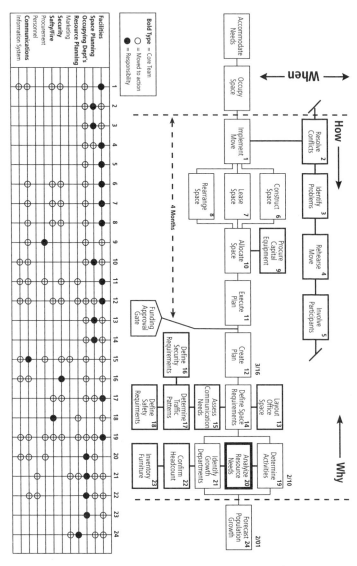

*Figure 17.    Facility planning FAST*

Note that each block is assigned a discrete number. How the blocks are numbered, whether sequentially or just the major logic blocks or all of the blocks, depends on the team's needs.

Viewing and analyzing downstream functions allowed the team to anticipate problems and resolve those issues early. This supported some of the team's "front-end loading" requirements. When the team analyzed the FAST model, it agreed that the choice of acquiring the required space cannot be resolved until the space requirements are defined (Box 14).

Team members identified four key completion dates (for blocks 12, 19, 20, 24). If those functions and their associated activities were satisfied by those dates, the assignment could be completed within the six months.

In business process studies, time is often more important than cost reduction. Time to market, process time and the time value of money are some key business issues where time is money. In addition to cost and time, FAST dimensions include, but are not limited to: responsibility, budgets, resource loading, expense allocation, determining value-added and non-value added functions, process phasing, funding stages, paperwork flow, capital equipment assessment, assigning target costs, establishing decision gates, positioning design reviews and many others.

In our case study, dimensioning provided a sensitivity matrix identifying the disciplines or departments involved in implementing the project. The bold type indicates the core team participation. The team discussed, analyzed and brainstormed each block to determine the best way to perform the functions and activities. It then decided which departments would be "moved to action" as a result of that block, indicated by an intersecting circle.

The team also decided which of the involved departments would be responsible for the performance described in that block, indicated by an intersecting black circle. Responsibility is one dimension. As discussed above, a great variety of dimensions and metrics can be used and displayed in constructing a sensitivity matrix.

The Funding Approval Gate symbol in Figure 17 illustrated when and how implementation funds would be available. The model shows that an implementation plan (Block 12) is required to justify project funding. In other FAST applications, the gate can represent design reviews, budget approval or any event where justification to proceed is required.

The project used for this case study achieved the move in five months and one week, without major incidents, well within budget constraints and judged successful by the people who were moved.

## Business Systems Re-Engineering and FAST

The FAST model has been used in business systems re-engineering projects to match functions to department charters and to determine direct responsibilities for those functions and others affected by the actions of the responsible groups. If a major reorganization is called for, a macro-level FAST model can be created with a team of senior managers to determine which functions to protect and which to separate from the organization under study without adversely affecting performance.

Most budgets are developed and justified by assessing the organization's level of activities. In terms of FAST, activities are the actions that implement functions. By analyzing and identifying the value-added function contributions of the operation under study, the organization can downsize by protecting and reinforcing charter functions, while divesting non-value-added activities from the organization. VM studies in business systems applications indicate that less than 35 percent of an organization's budget supports its major or charter functions. The remaining budget supports peripheral activities.

Goals can also be assigned to key functions. The dimensioned FAST model shows which goals are independent and which depend on other department inputs for their achievement.

FAST has proven to be an excellent planning tool and a way to present complex concepts in a logical business case form to senior management. A primary rule of the FAST process, disciplining the team participants to describe functions simply with active verbs and measurable nouns, is the key that makes multidiscipline teams work. The verb–noun rule acts as a common language resulting in effective communications across diverse disciplines. This allows marketing to communicate with product development, the physicist to explain his ideas functionally to the purchasing agent, and finance to relate the economic consequences of design decisions to the design engineer.

# Conclusions

Major breakthroughs in information technology and the growth of global competition are causing progressive managers to move away from Alfred Sloan's principles of management control and accountability. In its place, the small entrepreneurial-spirited business team has the advantage of rapid product development and deployment, at lower cost, accomplished with higher value-added ratios than in staff-heavy dominant competitors. VM provides the tools and disciplines the business teams need to help them achieve desired results.

To accomplish this worthy objective requires a process that allows and encourages interdisciplinary team members to communicate with each other to establish a common vision and make that vision a reality. The Function Analysis System Technique (FAST) is made to order as the methodology of choice.

# V.

## VALUE MANAGEMENT AND MARKETING

D EVELOPING, SORTING AND EVALUATING prelimi-
nary VM proposals that result from the speculation (creative) phase of the VM process will
ultimately determine the success or failure of the VE
effort. The Product Performance Profile discussed in this
chapter focuses on identifying those product attributes that
the market is willing to pay for that, in addition to price,
define "value." Once defined, these attributes are the best
criteria for evaluating the effectiveness of VE proposals.
As discussed in Chapter 1, analyze and resolve these
issues during the pre-event phase, before the start of a
VM project, not after screening and selecting the best
ideas and combining those ideas into proposals.

The Product Performance Profile process also allows
the producer to communicate clearly with the customer
to establish a clear vision of the customer's perception of
value. This places VM on the marketing side of the business, where "value" is ultimately determined.

# Know Your Customer

Selecting evaluation criteria is not only based on knowing your customer's requirements, but also understanding why the customer specifies those requirements. This leads to a better understanding of the customer's needs, wants and concerns. In his paper "Defining Great Products," Peter Marks said, "If team members do not have answers to questions like these, they are stuck in a bureaucratic mode. Their companies are not ready to harness the power of self-directed teams, nor are they well-equipped to build great products."[4]

The questions he refers to are:

1.  Who are your five top customers?

2.  How are they using your product?

3.  What is the number one reason your customers choose to buy your products?

4.  What unique customer-oriented value is your company trying to promote?

5.  What is your role in achieving this benefit to your customers?

6.  Why should your customers buy your product over your competitors'?

7.  What are the three best ways to keep or win new customers in the future?

## Know Your Competition

In conducting VE studies, it is important to know the competitors that will vie for the same customers. Developing the "best" product also requires understanding your competitors' positions.

The following questions stimulate discussion and direct team attention to the high-value functions and features that differentiate the company's product from competitors' products:

1.  Who are your two top competitors ?

2.  What is the primary reason that your customers choose competitors' products over yours?

3.  What are your competitors' strengths and weaknesses?

4.  How can you exploit your competitors' weaknesses?

5.  How can you overcome your competitors' strengths?

6.  How do their products compare in terms of:

    Cost?

    Availability?

    Reliability?

    Performance?

    Ease of use?

    Service?

If your market is price-sensitive, cost and its effect on price is important to the customer. But how important is it relative to other business considerations such as sales, profit, investment pay back and market share? If you believe that the customer determines the value of products and services, how important is price reduction relative to other attributes that customers consider valuable? This brings the following three key issues into focus:

1.    Which attributes shall we use in developing and evaluating VE proposals?

2.    What is the relative importance of these attributes?

3.    What is the best way to display the evaluation results?

## Product Performance Profile

The Product Performance Profile addresses these three issues in a structured format that applies across a broad market spectrum to improve the business practices within a business enterprise. Value practitioners should understand that all market areas have attributes that define buyer or owner patterns. These attributes should be incorporated into the product development and evaluation process.

For consistency, this chapter selects the consumer products market for discussing the Product Performance Profile concept. However, the same principles apply when confronting internal customers for improving business processes or evaluating a new technology.

The study of attributes is a five-step process that identifies, defines, measures and scales, relatively weights and displays the attributes.

## *Defining Value Attributes*

Peter Marks describes eight buying patterns or attributes that determine a product's success in consumer product markets.[5]

**Price**–Except in a commodity market, lowest price does not necessarily represent best value. The buyer perception of value assures that the price paid represents "the best" value.

**Availability**–This describes the when, where and how of the customer's want. Purchasing convenience, a helpful sales staff, and seller reputation are additional influences.

**Packaging**–Vision is the dominant sense making the product configuration or form a powerful buyer preference. The buyer sees the package or the product's physical form and geometry.

**Performance**–How well the product performs the user-wanted function(s).

**Ease of Use**–Engages all the senses (looks, feel, sound and smell). This attribute is intangible, but can represent the ultimate expression of understanding of what the customer really wants.

**Assurance**–Assured performance in terms of quality and reliability under foreseeable conditions. However, this attribute includes buyer confidence in addition to quality, reliability and service.

**Life-Cycle Costs**–The cost of ownership. This not only includes the expenses incurred following the purchase of the product, but also considers its resale value and disposal cost.

**Standards and Social Acceptance**–External influences that affect the purchase decision, including social factors, product evaluation publications, political pressures, status, image, industrial standards, and government regulations.

The above descriptions can be customized to better reflect a specific consumer market and the products being evaluated within those markets. Although the buying behavior pattern in the purchase of a camera and an automobile are about the same, the description of some attributes would differ as they relate to those products.

## Scaling Attributes

Once the Executive Review Board in the role of customer advocate and the VM teams have agreed on the selection and definitions of the attributes, it is necessary to tailor the attributes further by expressing them in measurable terms.

Not all attributes are quantitative, but it is important to have measurable attributes to support those goals that determine the success of the project. The following attributes have measurable terms: price, availability, performance, assurance, and life-cycle cost. Ease of use, packaging and standards and social acceptance are important attributes, but more often evaluated subjectively because they are difficult to express in quantitative terms.

## Slicing the Attributes

It is not necessary to define all attributes in a single measure. An attribute may have a number of measurable characteristics that collectively describe it. For example, the performance attribute for an automobile may include the following characteristics: speed, acceleration, road stability, cornering, noise and braking. Each of these characteristics can involve an in-depth study with a paired comparison and trade-off analysis to prioritize these characteristics. How fine to "slice" the attribute into how many characteristics depends on the objectives of the study and the unresolved problems or issues.

Experience shows that the quality of results do not improve much by performing a detailed analysis of every characteristic of an attribute. What is most important is knowledge about those characteristics that drive the attribute and defining them clearly so that all members of the VM team use the same definition and scale in evaluating the VE proposals.

Figure 18, for the controls architecture of a satellite communications system, illustrates how attributes are scaled from 1 (poor) to 10 (best). Scaling the attributes defines the range of each attribute that allows the analyst to evaluate the "goodness"of the proposal options. Attribute scales are case-specific, so the example is a guide and not a universal measure for all products. Furthermore,

## Project: Controls Architecture

| Attributes | 1 | 2 | 3 | 4 | 5 | 6 | 7 | 8 | 9 | 10 |
|---|---|---|---|---|---|---|---|---|---|---|
| **Packaging** (size) | 1.5 std.rack | | Std. rack | | .75 std.rack | | .5 std.rack | | | .25 std.rack |
| **Performance** (power watts) | 18 | 16 | 14 | 13 | 12 | 11 | 10 | 9 | 8 | 7 |
| **Ease of Use** | Reqrs. training | | | | Some instruct. needed | | | | | User friendly |
| **Assurances** (MTBF) | 12 mo. | | 16 mo. | | 24 mo. | | 36 mo. | | 48 mo. | 60 mo. |
| **Life Cycle** (X price) | 12X | 11X | 10X | 9.5X | 9X | 8.5X | 7.8X | 7.3X | 6.8X | 6.3X |
| **Standards/Social Acceptance** | Marginal min. std. | | Meet competi- tion | | | Accept. full stds. | | | | Greatly exceeds Reqrmnts. |
| **Price** (as % of system price) | 15 | 13 | 12 | 11 | 10 | 9 | 8 | 7 | 6 | 5 |
| **Availability** (months) | 18 | 16 | 14 | 12 | 10 | 9 | 8 | 7 | 6.5 | 6 |

*Figure 18.    Attribute scale*

even if another project has the same attributes as the illustration, the selection and scaling of attributes will change depending on their definition, project conditions, specific goals, the strength and weaknesses of those project attributes and other conditions.

## *Scaling the Attributes*

Although all selected attributes are important in the evaluation of VM proposals, they are not equally so. The customer best determines their relative importance. However, customers are often unavailable for VM projects that affect products or services. In this case, marketing, sales, and distribution sources can represent the customer well.

VM projects concerned with improving the company's technical or management processes have internal customer sources. As "customers," they are the best and often the only sources available to evaluate the relative importance of the attributes.

The paired comparison process that value practitioners commonly use is an excellent way for customer sources to determine the relative importance of attributes. It not only results in a priority list of attributes, but also assigns each attribute a numeric value or weight.

Figure 19 shows the attributes of a product, their total score (69) and their total weight (100), expressed as a percentage.

The paired comparison process allows the analysis of a number of attributes by considering only two attributes at a time. This avoids the confusion of attempting to juggle eight or ten attributes at the same time. For

|   | B | C | D | E | F | G | H | Attributes | Score | Weight in % |
|---|---|---|---|---|---|---|---|---|---|---|
| A | B2 | C3 | D3 | E3 | F2 | G3 | A2 | Price | 2 | 3 |
| | B | B3 | D3 | B3 | F3 | B3 | B2 | Availability | 13 | 19 |
| | | C | D3 | E2 | F3 | G1 | H2 | Packaging | 3 | 4 |
| | | | D | D3 | D3 | G1 | H2 | Performance | 15 | 22 |
| | | | | E | F3 | G2 | H1 | Ease of Use | 5 | 7 |
| | | | | | F | F3 | F3 | Assurances | 17 | 25 |
| | | | | | | G | H3 | Life Cycle Cost | 6 | 9 |
| | | | | | | | H | Standards | 8 | 11 |

Factor
1 Low
2 Medium
3 High

**Product:** Controls Architecture    **TOTAL**    69    100

*Figure 19.   Paired comparisons*

example, Price (A) is compared to Availability (B) by asking, "In this situation, which would you consider more important, Price or Availability?" Then, "How important would you consider the difference, Low (1), Medium (2) or High (3)?" Another way to determine relative importance is to ask, "Considering the current condition of the project, if you were given a lump sum of money, which of the two attributes would you improve?"

In this example, the team considered Availability more important than Price by a Medium (2) importance factor. This is indicated by noting "B2" in the first square. After all attributes have been paired and evaluated, the total number of points earned by each attribute is posted in the "Score" column, totaled and normalized to 100 percent.

During the pre-event phase, paired comparisons are used to resolve what attributes constitute project success, and to determine the definition of the attributes and how to evaluate them.

## *Graphically Displaying the Attributes*

Figure 20 shows the eight attributes displayed in a star configuration with each attribute divided into ten segments. These segments define the "goodness" of each attribute, with 10 being best and 1 being worst. Consider midpoint 5 as a market average unless a specific range is defined (such as illustrated in Figure 18).

Figure 21 focuses on one of the attributes in order to assign it a rating. The center circle represents unacceptable performance. Any attribute receiving a zero will cause the

**Product Performance Attribute**

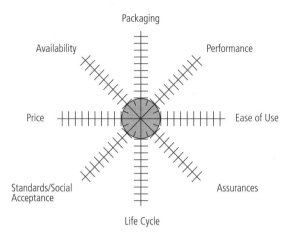

*Figure 20.    Star diagram*

entire project to fail, regardless of its weight. That's why the lowest attribute segment is one, not zero. For example, a project that receives a 10 in all but one attribute, but scored zero in Availability, would indicate that the project was not at all available and would therefore fail. Or, if the project received top scores, except for a zero in Ease of Use, then the zero would indicate that the team could not use the project and it would fail. A 1 indicates the worst possible acceptable condition for each attribute. Attributes cannot cross the minimum threshold. Any attribute that broaches the threshold will invalidate the entire proposal.

The Paired Comparison process normalizes the score to total 100 (see Figure 19, and Figure 22, row A) and divides each attribute into ten segments. The total number of available points (see Figure 22, row B) is 1,000 (100 X

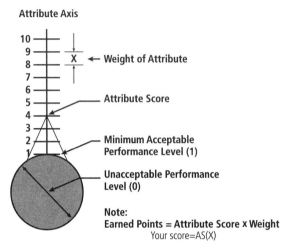

Attribute Axis

X ← Weight of Attribute

← Attribute Score

Minimum Acceptable
Performance Level (1)

Unacceptable Performance
Level (0)

Note:
Earned Points = Attribute Score x Weight
Your score=AS(X)

*Figure 21.    Attribute rating*

10). Filling in the weight values of each attribute in row A
shows that although the star is configured symmetrically,
each leg of the star (or attribute) has a different weight.
Although each attribute has ten increments, the values of
those increments differ with the importance or ranking of
the attributes. In Figures 19 and 22, the value or weight
of each Price increment is 3, compared to Assurances in
which the weight of each increment is 25. Because each
attribute has ten segments, the total available points that
any attribute can earn is the result of multiplying its
weight by 10. The result is posted in row B, Available
Points (see Figure 22).

Normalizing the weight creates a standard. Regardless of the type, number and individual weight of the
attributes, their total weights will always equal 100 and
the total available points will always equal 1,000.

**Product Performance Attribute**

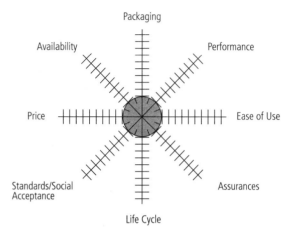

Score _____
Target ___700___                                      Project _____

| | Item | Price | Avail. | Package | Perform. | Ease/Use | Assur. | Life Cycl. | Standard | Total |
|---|---|---|---|---|---|---|---|---|---|---|
| A | Weight | 3 | 19 | 4 | 22 | 7 | 25 | 9 | 11 | 100 |
| B | Available Points | 30 | 190 | 40 | 220 | 70 | 250 | 90 | 110 | 1,000 |
| C | Your Score | | | | | | | | | |
| D | Competitor's Score | | | | | | | | | |
| | Delta (B) vs. (C) | | | | | | | | | |

*Figure 22.    Attribute grid*

## Evaluating Proposals

Figure 23 shows a completed attribute evaluation. As the team discusses and grades the merits of each proposal in terms of the governing attributes, scoring them from 1 to 10, the team marks the attribute grid on the graph to configure the points on the star. That score is multiplied by the attribute weight (row A) and the answer noted in

**Product Performance Profile**

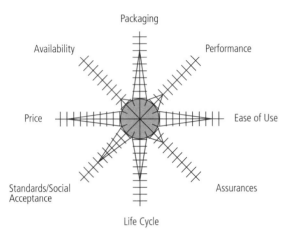

| | Item | Price | Avail. | Package | Perform. | Ease/Use | Assur. | Life Cycl. | Standard | **Total** |
|---|---|---|---|---|---|---|---|---|---|---|
| A | Weight | 3 | 19 | 4 | 22 | 7 | 25 | 9 | 11 | 100 |
| B | Available Points | 30 | 190 | 40 | 220 | 70 | 250 | 90 | 110 | 1,000 |
| C | Your Score | 27 | 38 | 32 | 66 | 63 | 75 | 45 | 66 | 412 |
| D | Competitor's Score | 12 | 76 | 32 | 132 | 56 | 120 | 54 | 77 | 559 |
| | Delta (C) vs. (D) | 15 | (38) | 0 | (66) | 7 | (45) | (9) | (11) | (147) |

**Score** 412
**Target** 700                                   **Project**

*Figure 23.    Evaluating attributes*

row C (Your Score). The Total column at the end of row C indicates the total number of points earned by the proposal, or the proposal's score. Row B, Available Points, shows the relative importance of each attribute by displaying the total number of points that an attribute can earn.

The team computes the Delta row by taking the difference between row B (Available Points) and row C (Your Score). This quickly shows the shortfall point value of the attribute. The team can evaluate their proposal against a target competitor (as in this example) by posting the competitor's attribute score in row D (Competitor's Score). Then use the Delta row to compare the team's proposed attribute performance to its competitor.

A positive value in a Delta box favors the team's proposal. A negative score favors the competitor. Using the competitor's score or a project target to determine an improvement objective, the team now has a visual illustration to gauge the effort needed to achieve project success.

Figure 23 represents a star diagram taken from the VE study of the controls system architecture, part of a large-capital communications system. Price received a low weight because project management ruled that the controls system cost should not exceed 15 percent of the total system cost (or price), which was assigned a very conservative target cost. This reduced the significance of the price attribute.

The 15 percent price limit also determined increment number 1 on the price attribute scale. The team decided that the most optimistic cost would be 5 percent of the system cost, which established increment number 10. The range from 5 to 15 percent was divided between the ten-increment spread, giving a weighted value to each increment on the attribute scale (see Figure 18).

Packaging also received a low weight because the controls were integrated into the total system. The functional response and visual effects of the controls subjectively determined the evaluation. Also, Ease of Use was rated relatively low because industrial ergonomic standards determine the type and placement of controls.

However, Assurance, Performance, Availability and Standards were rated relatively high because they represent the primary customer concerns in this market area.

Figure 24 shows the results of a VM effort to achieve the target score of 700 points.

An overlay of the two star diagrams shows the base case condition compared to the potential results of the VM

**Product Performance Profile**

**Score** _716_
**Target** _700_                                                   Project _____

| | Item | Price | Avail. | Package | Perform. | Ease/Use | Assur. | Life Cycl. | Standard | Total |
|---|---|---|---|---|---|---|---|---|---|---|
| A | Weight | 3 | 19 | 4 | 22 | 7 | 25 | 9 | 11 | 100 |
| B | Available Points | 30 | 190 | 40 | 220 | 70 | 250 | 90 | 110 | 1,000 |
| C | Your Score | 6 | 57 | 36 | 198 | 56 | 225 | 72 | 66 | 716 |
| D | Competitor's Score | | | | | | | | | |
| | Delta (B) vs. (C) | 24 | 133 | 4 | 22 | 14 | 25 | 18 | 44 | 248 |

*Figure 24.    A value improved proposal*

team. This view reveals the result of trading off attributes to improve the overall goodness of the product offering.

## Setting Targets

Note that this controls architecture proposal earned a total of 716 points out of a possible 1000, against an aggressive target of more than 700 points. Judging from the more than 50 diverse case studies where the Product Performance Profile was used for new product development assignments, a target of 550 to 650 points seems to be the entry level of proposal acceptability. However, the stakeholders or Executive Review Board should determine the target as part of the Paired Comparison process. Establishing a target for total earned points allows the team to revise and upgrade their proposals by focusing on improving the high-weight attributes.

In the above example, the diagram indicates that, before the VM study, the product did fairly well in the Price, Standards, Life Cycle, Ease of Use and Packaging attributes. However, the total earned points of 412 fell short of the 700-point target. The reason for the low score becomes apparent when looking at the attribute weights. The more important, highly-weighted attributes received poor scores.

### *Trading off Attributes*

Focusing on improving the high-weight attributes such as Performance, Assurance and Availability could earn the needed points, even if it requires a trade-off against the other attributes. For example, if Performance improved from 3 to 7 (or +4) and Assurances improved from 2 to 5 (or +3), but it required a higher price that reduced the Price grid from 9 to 6 (or -3), the result would be a net +154 points (or, [4(22)] + [3(25)] - [3(3)] =154). That raises the total earned points to 566 (412 + 154). Additional trade-offs in this direction could conceivably result in achieving the target value. Because each attribute has a floor or a low-end threshold, improving high-weighted attributes by trading off against low-weighted attributes is a viable approach as long as the low-end threshold of the attribute isn't broached.

## Conclusions

Developing creative ideas and proposals is an important part of the VM equation. Equally important is to ensure that the evaluation of VM proposals is based on those parameters that define success. The evaluation parameters must reflect the attributes judged important by those who also judge value.

And the ultimate value judge is the customer.

# References

1. Monroe, Kent B. "Pricing: Making Profitable Decisions," *The Conference Board,* 1979.

2. Ibid.

3. Bytheway, Charles, W. "The Creative Aspects of FAST Diagramming," *SAVE Proceedings,* Vol. VI, 1979, pp. 301–312.

4. Marks, Peter. "Defining Great Products," *Design Insight,* 1991.

5. Miles, Lawrence D. *Techniques of Value Analysis and Engineering.* Second edition. McGraw Hill, Inc., 1972.

# FURTHER READING

Kaufman, J. Jerry. "The Power of FAST in Value Management," *SAE Technical Paper Series #970761*. SAE International, February, 1997.

Kaufman, J. Jerry. *Value Engineering for the Practitioner*. North Carolina State University, Raleigh, North Carolina, 1985.

Miles, Lawrence D. *Techniques of Value Analysis and Engineering*. Second Edition. McGraw-Hill, Inc., 1972.

Fallon, Carlos. *Value Analysis*. Second revised edition. Wiley-Interscience, 1980.

Akiyama, Kaneo. *Function Analysis. Systematic Improvement of Quality and Performance*. Productivity Press, Inc., 1991.

For additional reading references on Value Management, contact SAVE International, 60 Revere Drive, Suite 500, Northbrook, IL 60062. Telephone: (847) 480-1730, Fax: (847) 480-9282

# About the Author

Jerry Kaufman, founder of J. J. Kaufman Associates, Inc., a value management services company, has over 40 years of design engineering, value management and corporate management experience in the industrial, electronic, processes, services and aerospace markets.

Formerly on the corporate staff of Cooper Industries as director of Value Management, his experience includes 25 years of progressively responsible management positions involving products, processes, and business management. Jerry is a past president and past certified value specialist (CVS), board chairman of the Society of American Value Engineers (SAVE International), and is internationally known and honored in his field. He has been cited in "Engineers of Distinction" by the Engineers Joint Council in 1973, received the Meritorious Service award, and is a Fellow and Life Member of SAVE. In 1980, he was awarded the Presidential Citation by the Society for Japanese Value Engineering for his contributions in establishing Value Engineering in Japan. The American Association of Cost Engineers (AACE) recognized Jerry as their Speaker of the Year for the period 1989–1990.

In 1994, SAVE presented the Lawrence D. Miles award, its highest achievement award, to Jerry for his many contributions to the field of Value Engineering.

Jerry joins a select group of four recipients to receive this rarely presented award since its inception 20 years ago.

In addition to numerous papers presented internationally, Jerry is a co-author of two books and has written a third book titled, *Value Engineering for the Practitioner,* published by North Carolina State University (NCSU). Jerry taught Value Management in series of industrial extension courses for NCSU and McGill University's Management Institute in Montreal, Canada. Jerry has also conducted Value Management seminars in Canada, Europe, England, Japan and Korea. As president of J. J. Kaufman Associates, he has provided consultant services and conducted Value Management workshops related to product development, manufacturing, process improvement, total quality management, and organization effectiveness (business systems re-engineering) to many multi-national corporations around the world.

J.Jerry Kaufman
12006 Indian Wells Drive
Houston, TX 77066
Telephone: (281) 444-6887
Fax: (281) 444-6880
e-mail: jkaufman@flash.net